W9-AZA-778

thrift SHOPPING

Discovering Bargains and Hidden Treasures

SANDY DONOVAN

TWENTY-FIRST CENTURY BOOKS / MINNEAPOLIS

Acknowledgments:
The publisher wishes to thank Kris Vetter for
making the crafts on pages 45, 47, and 49.

Twenty-First Century Books
A division of Lerner Publishing Group, Inc.
241 First Avenue North
Minneapolis, MN 55401 USA

For updated reading levels and more information, look up this title at www.lernerbooks.com.

Main body text set in Adobe Garamond Pro Regular 11/16.
Typeface provided by Adobe Systems.

Library of Congress Cataloging-in-Publication Data

Donovan, Sandra, 1967–
    Thrift shopping : discovering bargains and hidden treasures / by Sandy Donovan.
        pages   cm
    Includes bibliographical references and index.
    ISBN 978-1-4677-5783-6 (lib. bdg. : alk. paper)
    ISBN 978-1-4677-6310-3 (EB pdf)
    1. Shopping—Juvenile literature. 2. Thrift shops—Juvenile literature. 3. Purchasing—Juvenile
literature. I. Title.
TX335.5.D66 2015
381'.19—dc23   2014020885

Manufactured in the United States of America
1 – BP – 12/31/14

Contents

Thrifting is an affordable and fun way to expand any wardrobe, whether casual or upscale.

INTRODUCTION
What Is Thrift Shopping?

Thrifting is hot. It's a trend with teens, adults, and even superrich celebs. Rappers Macklemore and Ryan Lewis made some serious dough when their megahit "Thrift Shop" went to the top of the pop charts in 2013. Even as a wealthy star, Macklemore continues to make fashion statements with thrift-shop finds. Style-conscious actress and singer Jada Pinkett Smith and her fashion-forward daughter, Willow, are often spotted hitting the thrift shops in Santa Monica, California. Singer-songwriters Janelle Monáe and Zooey Deschanel love thrifting too.

So what's the scoop on thrifting? You probably have a pretty good idea of what it is. Thrifting is shopping for clothing, jewelry, accessories, furniture, gifts, collectibles, and other goods that have been donated new or already owned and used by someone else. At a wide range of outlets—including thrift shops, consignment stores, vintage boutiques, garage sales, flea markets, and online sites—thrift shoppers pay a lot less than if they were buying the items brand new. But any veteran thrift shopper will tell you that there's much more to thrifting than simply finding an awesome bargain. There's the sense of adventure, the exhilaration of scoring just what you were hunting for, and often the fun of a surprise find.

Read on to find out why so many people are enthusiastic about the art of thrift shopping—and then settle in for some tips on how to make the most of your own thrift-shop expeditions.

Garage sales and flea markets offer amazing thrift-shopping opportunities for everything from clothing and housewares to furniture and sporting goods.

CHAPTER 1
Why Thrift?

Thrifting was originally a way for people to buy basic necessities that they might not otherwise have been able to afford. Thrift stores were generally run by charitable organizations that wanted to help people in need and to raise money for good causes through thrift-store sales. For example, one of the earliest thrift shops was started in the late 1800s by a society for the blind in London, England. By the late twentieth century, thrifting had gone mainstream, and in the twenty-first century, thrift sales are rising every year. In fact, thrifting is the subject of reality shows, fashion magazine spreads, and more than one hit pop song. Shopping for bargains has become a favorite pastime of teens, adults, and even major fashionistas. Many people like thrifting as a way to support an organization whose mission they believe in. Others like the idea of going green through thrifting. Purchasing secondhand items is a great way to recycle and reduce waste.

So what exactly is the big deal about thrifting? Why are so many people hooked? Thrifters give five reasons for getting addicted to this pastime.

Reason to Thrift #1: Save Money

No doubt about it. It's cheaper—way cheaper—to buy used than new. Thrift-shop goods are usually priced anywhere from 50 percent to 95 percent less than their new counterparts. A pair of jeans that costs one hundred dollars new can often be found for approximately ten to forty dollars secondhand. Sometimes they may go for even less, depending on their condition, what kind of store is selling them, and other factors. Buying used can save lots of $$$.

If the thought of saving money makes you yawn, here's another way to think about the value of thrifting: more bling for your buck. Saving money through thrift shopping allows buyers to purchase a few more must-haves. Rather than spending a chunk of change on only one pair of new shoes, you could go home with two pairs of shoes, a pair of jeans, and an awesome hat to top off the look. How's that for thrifty shopping?

Reason to Thrift #2: Find Unique Clothes or Satisfy a Creative Urge

Many thrifters love the chance to score vintage, unusual, or one-of-a kind items. Be honest, when someone shows up at school in a new shirt, jacket, or pair of shoes, they're often similar to what other people

Thrifting with a friend or family member is a good way to get a second opinion on something you're not sure about. And it can be a fun way to spend time together.

are wearing, right? It's even pretty obvious where the person purchased the item too. Buying from thrift stores, on the other hand, offers the opportunity to find something truly unique or even to uncover a designer-label bargain. It's one way to land an item that no one at school has ever seen before. Now that's trendsetting!

For shoppers who like to apply creative talents to the way they dress, decorate a room, or assemble handcrafted gifts and other items, a thrift store can be the go-to spot for standout treasures. Do you like the styles of the 1950s, the 1960s, or the 1970s? A secondhand or vintage store, a garage sale, and online sites are great places to look. Obsessed with do-it-yourself projects? You'll find the raw materials you need—at a price you'll like—for gifts, accessories, household decorations, and more.

Reason to Thrift #3: Save the World

Okay, maybe thrift-shop purchases aren't going to save the world, but they can help lessen the footprint we humans leave behind. These days, manufacturing new items is a global affair. Many goods available for sale in the United States are produced in sweatshops in poor nations of the world, where people—even children—work for long hours in unsafe, unhealthy conditions for very little pay. Factories that produce the goods may be using unsafe chemicals in the manufacturing process or in the goods themselves. Many factories and the vehicles that ship the goods to market rely on carbon-based fuels, such as coal and petroleum, which contribute to global warming. Thrift shopping helps reduce the wasteful production of new goods. It's also a form of recycling. Every item purchased in a thrift shop is another item that doesn't end up in a landfill.

Reason to Thrift #4: Have Fun with Friends

Some super-serious thrifters like to go it alone. But many thrift shoppers say that setting out with a few friends for an afternoon of digging and diving—yes, you sometimes have to dig and dive for gems—is their favorite part.

Thrifting can be a great team sport, whether the group is on the hunt for the same item or has different bullet points on the shopping list. It's as easy as picking a time and a place—and letting the shopping unfold. Having friends along to give the thumbs-up or thumbs-down can be super helpful. It's especially useful to thrift with someone who has experience and can point out the pros and cons of a potential purchase. Some thrifters just like to tag along with a group for the fun of being with friends, even when they aren't planning to shop for themselves.

Reason to Thrift #5: Enjoy the Thrill of the Hunt!

The ultimate thrifting thrill? Uncovering a real treasure. The awesome find can be a perfectly broken-in pair of cowboy boots or a super-fashionable designer dress. Or it can be the truly unexpected find: a limited-release vinyl record you never even knew your favorite band put out or the most standout, sparkling fake diamond you've ever seen.

Quick Quiz: Are You Ready to Thrift?

Ready to give thrifting a try? Take this short quiz.

1. Say you need just the right new outfit to wear to the party of the year—and you only have $20 to make it happen. Which of the following sounds like the best option for getting yourself party-ready?

   a. Digging through the everyday clothes at the back of your closet to find something that will work.

   b. Heading to the mall to scour the sale racks.

   c. Hitting a thrift shop for a head-to-toe makeover.

2. You've been noticing other guys wearing cool 1950s'-style, skinny-collared jackets. You think you'd like to give the look a try, but you're worried you may look ridiculous. Which sounds like the most risk-free way to try out the look?

   a. Blowing your savings on a look-alike designer jacket.

   b. Rejecting the jacket idea altogether. Why take the risk on a look that may not work for you?

   c. Checking out your neighborhood vintage store to find a true 1950s'-style jacket at a fraction of the price.

3. Lately, you've been really concerned about the environment. Which of these options sounds like a realistic, concrete way to help the planet?

a. Decide you're never, ever going to travel by anything other than your own power. No cars, planes, buses, or trains.

b. Take a pledge to start informing your friends and neighbors about the impact of their carbon footprint.

c. Make an effort to buy as many secondhand goods as you can.

If you chose C for all the questions, you are a prime thrifting candidate!

Secondhand clothing shops can be a perfect solution if you're looking for fun party dresses or evening wear at a good price.

Thrift shops come in all shapes and sizes. This store offers a mix of antique housewares and more up-to-date accessories. Part of the fun of thrifting is finding great things in unanticipated places.

CHAPTER 2
Where to Thrift

Ready to hit the stores or go online for a thrifting adventure? First, take a minute to think about where exactly to do your thrift shopping. Lots of different types of sellers offer a wide range of items for sale. Some are known for having the least expensive goods. Others have a reputation for the best vintage selections. Some are permanent stores with dependable, set hours. Others are pop-up opportunities that serious thrifters don't want to miss. Some places are well organized and suitable for a quick drop-in shopping blitz. Others are jam-packed with unsorted items, calling for a careful plan of attack.

Nonprofit Thrift Stores

Think Goodwill, Salvation Army, or Volunteers of America (VoA). These classic thrift stores are run by nonprofit organizations to raise money to support a specific mission. Most operate in the same way. They take donations of clothing, household goods, furniture, sporting gear, books, CDs, DVDs, and other used items or collectibles and sell them for low prices. The profits help support the work the organization does in the community. Many of these stores use volunteer workers to sort through the donations or to staff the shop as salespeople. Because the organizations get their inventory from donations (that is—for free!) and some of their labor from volunteers (also free), the stores can sell items for low prices and still make plenty of money.

That's not to say that all nonprofit thrift stores are alike. Some are huge organizations, with storefronts that span entire city blocks. These stores tend to be affiliated with large national or international nonprofits. Other thrift stores are tiny one-room shops that support small local charities or religious groups. Each nonprofit thrift store has its own personality, reflected in what it offers for sale. Some sell only clothing or only household goods. Others sell nothing larger than a toaster. Somes sell cars and boats.

Selection and pricing at nonprofit thrift shops vary a lot too. Stores that are in middle- or upper-income suburban areas tend to have broad selections of newer items, often in new or nearly new condition. But they can also have the highest prices. In smaller towns or lower-income areas, you might find much lower prices. You might also find less selection. This isn't always true, however. Some cities have thrift shops with extensive selections and bargain prices, no matter what neighborhood. Ask around and do a little online research to find out where the best thrift stores are in your area.

The bottom line? Compared to other types of thrift stores, nonprofits offer the most hit-or-miss experience. You may have to sift through a lot of junk—or go to the same store more than once—before finding something really awesome for really cheap.

The Biggest Nonprofit Thrift Stores in the United States and Canada

Here's a list of the largest American and Canadian nonprofit organizations that support thrift stores, with a short description of each organization's mission:

The American Cancer Society's Discovery Shop Thrift Stores. This US organization, founded in 1913, is dedicated to eliminating cancer. Since 1974 its Discovery Shop stores have sold clothing, accessories, jewelry, furniture, artwork, antiques, collectibles, and other household items to support its work.

Arc Thrift Stores. Arc was founded in 1950 as an advocacy group for people with intellectual and developmental disabilities. Many of its chapters operate thrift stores to raise money for the organization's programming. Arc stores sell clothing, toys, accessories, books, sporting and household goods, and very small furniture.

Disabled American Veterans (DAV) Thrift Stores. Founded in 1920 by a group of disabled veterans, the DAV supports veterans and their families. DAV stores specialize in clothing, jewelry, furniture, bikes, books, CDs, and other small items.

Goodwill Stores. The retail arm of Goodwill Industries International was founded in 1902 by a Methodist minister. Goodwill collected clothing and household items, trained unemployed people to repair the goods, and then sold or donated the items. Twenty-first-century Goodwill stores follow the same model, offering a wide range of items, from clothing and footwear to household goods, books, toys, and sporting equipment.

Saint Vincent de Paul Thrift Stores. Started in Paris, France, in 1833 by the Catholic Church, the Society of Saint Vincent de Paul quickly spread to the United States. In the twenty-first century, the organization operates thrift stores in the United States, Canada, and Australia to support low-income families and individuals worldwide. The stores sell donated clothing, accessories, toys, and sporting and household goods, as well as used vehicles, including cars, trucks, boats, motor homes, and motorcycles.

Salvation Army Thrift Stores. The Salvation Army was founded in London in 1865 by a Methodist minister. Its thrift stores raise money to support homeless shelters, global disaster relief, and other poverty relief efforts. The stores primarily sell donated used items such as clothing, housewares, and toys.

Volunteers of America Thrift Stores. Voluneers of America was founded in 1896 by the son and the daughter-in-law of the founder of the Salvation Army to help low-income people in New York. The nonprofit serves four hundred communities in the United States. Many local chapters operate thrift stores that sell donated clothes, furniture, household goods, toys, sporting equipment, and vehicles.

The Goodwill thrift shop enterprise is a multi-billion-dollar industry that uses most of its earnings to provide employment, training, and support services to millions of people in need.

Insider Tip: Get Outside Your Comfort Zone

To find a wider array of selection, try visiting thrift shops in areas not known for thrift-shop cool. Stores in locations that are the home base of hipsters, college students, and other frequent thrifters are often picked over. Demand for thrift goods in these neighborhoods is high, so the shops are likely to have higher prices. Thrifters who get outside the hottest thrifting neighborhoods are far more likely to come across truly unique pieces—and for a lower price too!

For-Profit Thrift and Used-Goods Stores

Not all large thrift stores are connected to nonprofit organizations. Some popular chains sell used items to make a profit. Depending on location, these stores may have slightly higher-quality merchandise than some nonprofit stores. And they may be stricter about the quality of items they sell, offering only items that are in working condition and free of tears, stains, or cracks. For example, some stores offer only items that are one to three years old. This means items at for-profit outlets may be slightly newer or in better condition, but the prices are likely to be slightly higher.

For-profit businesses often get their inventory by buying used clothing, sporting equipment, household goods, small furniture, and other items directly from the previous owners. Owners receive a small payment up front. Some stores specialize in certain products. For example, a used sporting goods store might carry equipment and gear for golf, tennis, hockey, skiing, and other activities. A secondhand clothing store might focus on teen trends, special-occasion wear, or maternity clothes. For many of these stores, a basic rule of thumb is that they sell the items for about one-third of the original retail price. The original owner then earns about one-third of the thrift price, once the item is sold.

The bottom line? For-profit thrift stores usually sell fairly recent, gently used items for a low price. The price may not be as low as a charity-based thrift shop, but it may be easier to find what you're looking for with less digging. On the other hand, for-profit outlets have usually picked out the most valuable items to sell at a higher price—or to an antique or vintage dealer—so it's unusual to find a true diamond in the rough here.

Consignment Stores

A consignment shop functions as a dealer for people who want to sell their used clothing to earn some money. These shops often look similar to thrift stores but tend to specialize in more upscale clothing, accessories, and special-event attire such as prom wear. Here's the deal: a person brings good-condition, brand-name clothes to a consignment shop and agrees to the price for which the store will try to sell the items. If the store sells any of the items, it takes a percentage of the selling price as a fee and gives the rest to the seller. If an item doesn't sell within a specified time—often just weeks—the price is cut in half. Then the store and the seller earn a smaller profit. If, after another set time, an item still hasn't sold, it goes back to the seller—or if the seller agrees, the shop donates the item to charity.

Many consignment stores have strict policies about the brands they will sell. Some focus only on exclusive designer brands, and some focus on more middle-of-the-road brands that are easy to find—at full price, of course—in malls. Some consignment shops offer a mix of both. Many will only sell clothes that are less than a year or two old and have no rips or stains whatsoever. Because the items are usually of much higher quality than at thrift stores, shoppers expect to pay a higher price. They can also expect to find more recent styles.

The bottom line? Pricing is a little higher at a consignment store than at a thrift store. But if you're looking for designer brands and recent styles of high quality, you're more likely to find them here.

Vintage and Antique Shops

Like consignment shops, vintage and antique shops are privately run stores that sell previously owned goods. But they don't sell just any used goods. These stores typically have more specialized selections than classic thrift stores do. They also tend to be more expensive than thrift stores are. *Vintage* usually refers to clothing and accessories from previous decades, while *antique* typically refers to historic furniture and other household goods. Both types of stores do a little more work for the shopper than thrift stores do. Buyers for vintage and antique shops are selective, often scouring flea markets, estate sales, garage sales, auctions, and specialty sales looking for specific types or brands of older items. And the sales staff is often willing to work with buyers to find just the right piece of clothing or furniture.

Many vintage and antique stores specialize in a certain period, such as clothes from the 1950s or furniture from the early 1900s. Some vintage and antique clothing stores have a wider range of goods. Prices and quality can vary dramatically at vintage and antique stores, depending on how specialized the selection is and how much personalized service the staff offers its clients. For instance, vintage clothing stores in college and tourist neighborhoods are likely to be very similar to classic thrift stores. Quality won't necessarily be top of the line, but prices will be very affordable. On the other hand, a classy, upscale vintage clothing store selling little black dresses from top designers of the 1950s and the 1960s may charge hundreds—even thousands—of dollars for each piece, especially if the shop is in a trendy neighborhood. Though the price tag may be high for some items, the value of the item in another setting, such as an auction, could be many times higher.

The bottom line? If you're searching for unique or specialized items—and especially if you want them from a certain era—a vintage clothing shop or antique furniture gallery may be just the ticket for you. Expect to pay more, and also expect to sift through fewer items to find exactly what you're looking for. Just remember—at almost all secondhand stores, all sales are final.

Rummage and Garage Sales

Some people think of rummage and garage sales as the ultimate thrifting experience. These are sales organized by individuals, institutions, or groups of friends or neighbors to sell their own used items. They sometimes even sell new items the owner simply hasn't gotten around to wearing or pulling out of the box or assembling. Rummage and garage sales can be just the place to find clothing, sports gear, toys, household items, jewelry, books and records—and occasionally a truly valuable piece of artwork or historic memorabilia. Sometimes the seller may not know what the piece is really worth and just wants to get rid of it to clean out an attic or a basement crammed with "junk."

You can tell a lot about these venues by what they're called. For example, at a rummage or garage sale, shoppers generally have to pick through a lot of items—often unsorted. Usually individuals and neighborhoods use the term *garage sale*, while churches and other organizations use the term *rummage sale*. Items at both are generally, though not always, priced to move. Clothing is often priced under one dollar, and household goods are just a few dollars.

Yard sales and garage sales typically get rolling early in the morning. You'll find the best selection if you show up right away. But you may be able to bargain for better pricing later in the day.

Location and timing play a huge role in gem-finding success at a garage sale. Here's the deal: at these sales, people are unloading items they no longer want. But they also want to make at least a modest profit. In general, sales in higher-income neighborhoods are more likely to sell newer items in better condition than in lower-income communities. On the other hand, the items may be a little pricier because the original value of an item is typically higher. But if you hit a garage or rummage sale toward the end of the day—when the seller is tired and wants to wrap up—it can be easy to make a bargain for a much lower price.

The bottom line? If you're truly in it for the thrill of the hunt and love to dig through junk for a bargain treasure, garage sales and rummage sales are right up your alley. You'll spend time sifting through stuff, and you may go home empty-handed. But if you do it often enough, you may find something you really love—and you may be able to take it home for fifty cents.

Auctions, Estate Sales, and Flea Markets

These are the pop-up shops of the thrifting world. Auctions are one-time events where goods are sold to the highest bidder. There's usually a formal process to follow. Customers sign in and are assigned auction numbers. A professional auctioneer announces each item and sets a minimum bid. Customers raise a hand or an auction sign to up the bid. Sometimes customers get into a bidding war and prices go quite high. Other times only one or two people place a bid and an item sells quickly at a reasonable price. Either way, the highest bidder wins the item.

Auctions have personalities, just like thrift shops. Some auctions sell cars or large farm equipment. Others sell art or the content of abandoned storage rental units. Auctions that sell off the property of someone who has recently died are often called estate sales. These can be opportunities to find vintage clothing and accessories, furniture, art, and small household goods. Announcements for local estate sales show up online or in local newspapers.

Unlike auctions or estate sales, flea markets are not pop-up events. Many cities and towns have a particular area where flea markets set up every day or every weekend. Sellers usually pay a small fee to the organizers and

Look for flea markets in big cities and small towns. Some offer very unique items, while others sell a range of everyday ware. You can sometimes bargain with vendors at flea markets too.

then set up their own booths or tables. Typical flea market items include jewelry, vintage clothes, art, toys, vinyl records, books, furniture, silverware, and other household goods. Some sellers are willing to bargain over prices, while some won't budge on pricing at all.

The bottom line? Whatever they sell, flea markets and auctions can be colorful spots for shopping expeditions. You might uncover a true gem, or you might just have fun marveling at the unique collections you find. And you can put your bargaining and bidding skills to work!

Online

Looking for some serious bargains but don't feel like hitting the shops? You can successfully thrift shop from your computer, tablet, or smart phone. Many major nonprofit thrift shops, as well as an increasing number of smaller independent stores, have websites. Others use their Facebook pages to let customers get a peek at or even buy items without coming to the store. And, of course, there are always sites such as eBay and Craigslist, two of the Web's largest movers of secondhand items. Both allow you to search for specific items. In general, Craigslist is a place for local sellers who expect buyers to pick up purchases, while eBay sellers are national—or even international—and plan to ship purchases to buyers.

Get started with online thrifting by Googling "online thrift store" or by visiting eBay.com or your local craigslist.com site. Check with a parent or a guardian to make sure you can make online purchases. Most sites require buyers to be over the age of eighteen. An adult can also help you verify that the seller is legitimate. Many sites use an auction format, where the buyer bids on items and waits to see if other sellers bid higher. If they do, you get the chance to increase your bid. After an agreed-upon time, the highest bidder wins the item for the bid. Other online sites sell items for a set price, just as in a store. Either way, you'll need an adult to handle your online payment. Every seller also has slightly different shipping policies and prices,

Beyond eBay

Online thrift shopping is taking off. Besides traditional sites such as eBay, Etsy, and Craigslist, a wide range of secondhand online retailers is enticing millions of users. The leading site so far is **POSHMARK**. It works like eBay and Instagram combined, with users posting photos in a virtual closet that shoppers can browse and choose from. Visitors can also like and comment each other's closets. In addition, through its mobile app, Poshmark hosts **POSH PARTIES** centered around certain trends.

Poshmark isn't the only player, though. Other popular secondhand online retailers include **BIB & TUCK**, **WALK IN MY CLOSET**, **SHOP HERS**, **TWICE**, **THREADFLIP**, and **TRADESY**. Offerings range from high-fashion designer labels to everyday street wear—all at reduced prices. Some of the sites have online trunk shows to preview selections, while others have personalized concierge-style shopping services. To use these online retailers, shoppers must generally be eighteen or older, so ask an adult to help if you want to shop or sell online through these sites.

so check them out before you buy. If you are responsible for picking up a purchase, make sure you choose a public site during the day. And bring an adult with you.

Why thrift online? To benefit from a broader selection of items more quickly and with the convenience of one-stop shopping. You can compare prices for similar items across different sellers. You can also read customer reviews to get a better sense of how reputable the seller is and whether the deal is a good one or not. If you live in an area without many thrift stores, you can expand your options by shopping online. The downside of online thrifting is that you can't see or hold or try on the items. And you don't get the immediate satisfaction of taking your purchases home with you right away.

The bottom line? Online thrifting can be a great choice if you're looking for a particular item or a specific style. But if thrifting is all about the experience and hanging out with friends, skip the Web and hit the shops.

When thrifting for clothes, be sure to inspect each item for rips, stains, discoloration, or missing pieces that you might have to replace yourself.

CHAPTER 3
What to Thrift

Ready to hit the thrift store? What exactly can shoppers expect to find? The short answer is anything and everything. Popular categories include clothing, footwear, jewelry, handbags, furniture, sporting goods, vinyl records, small household goods, and gifts. Here are some tips about what to look for and how to assess quality.

Clothing

At the top of most thrifters' shopping lists is clothing. You name it—jeans, dress pants, shirts and sweaters, dresses, skirts, suits and jackets, coats, formal wear, swimming suits, and more—you can find it all at a thrift store.

It's often easier to shop for clothes at a thrift store than at most mall or department stores. That's because many thrift stores organize their collections by the type of item rather than scattering similar types of clothing throughout the store. Looking for jeans? Head to the jeans rack, where they're all lined up by size. Want a long-sleeved T-shirt? Hit the T-shirt rack. Sometimes the store separates items by color as well.

Use these tips to become an expert clothing thrifter:

Think about an item's overall quality. A shopper doesn't have to know everything about fancy designer labels to be able to spot good quality. A well-made piece of clothing has generous seams and fits comfortably. The fabric is usually made from natural fibers such as cotton, wool, or silk—or some combination of natural fibers—and feels good to the touch. It drapes, or hangs, nicely on the body, and its colors are rich. Be on the lookout for cheaply or quickly made items—for instance, clothing with gaping or irregular seams or with super-thin fabric that won't last long. Fabrics made from artificial fibers, such as polyester, can be another sign of lower-quality clothing. Check for tears, holes, or stains too. Some shops sell clean, spotless clothes, while others do not. Ask a salesclerk if the clothes have been washed. If they haven't, plan to wash them at home. And look at labels. Clothing that is made in very poor parts of the world, such as Bangladesh and Cambodia, are often not made as well as items that are made in the United States or in Western Europe. Labels will tell you about the fabric and who the designer is.

- **Don't worry about small flaws.** While it's generally wise to avoid buying a piece of clothing with a huge rip or a giant stain in a super-visible spot, a missing button or a small tear in a seam isn't a smart reason to pass over something you love. It's easy to stitch up a seam at home and to sew on a new button—or to replace them all with a different color or style! If you don't know how to do this, ask a friend or an adult to help.

- **Think twice about light colors.** Carefully inspect any piece of clothing that is white, yellow, or a pastel color. Small stains or discoloration—sometimes just from the age of the fabric—show

Planning to dress for a theme party or looking for just the right retro look? A thrift shop is likely to have just what you need.

up more on lighter colors than on darker fabrics. And the stains are often difficult, if not impossible, to remove, even with specialty laundry products. But if the discoloration is in a hard-to-see spot, such as an inside hem or lining, many shoppers will choose to buy the item anyway. Who's going to see the imperfection?

- **Pay attention to when the item was made.** In general, clothing made in the 1980s or earlier is of higher quality and holds up better through many washes and wears. In those days, fabrics and color dyes were made to last. It's not always easy to tell when something was manufactured, but if you recognize a style or a look from one of the big stores at the mall, chances are the piece was made recently and may not be as sturdy as a similar piece from an earlier decade. Of course, if you're shopping for vintage clothes, the selection will automatically be from another era. But beware. Some vintage clothes may not have traveled well through the years and may have rips, stains, or weak spots. An item may have hard-to-remove odors from having been stored in damp, smelly basements or in hot, humid attics for a long time.

- **Watch for pilling on knit sweaters and cotton shirts.** You've seen pills: those tiny clumps of fibers that stick out in an unsightly manner on sweaters and other knit materials. Pilling can be a sign of a poor-quality fabric or sometimes just age. Once a fabric pills, the pilling will get worse with wear. A good rule of thumb is that the softer a sweater is, the more likely it will be to pill. More tightly knit garments tend to pill less. In addition, natural fibers tend to pill less than polyester and other artificial fibers. If you're looking at a sweater that has obviously been around for a long time, has no pills, and is made from a natural fiber, you're probably safe. But if you're looking at artificial fabrics, pay attention to pill potential.

- **Look for one-of-a-kind items to pair with things you already own.** Do a quick closet inventory before shopping. Already have plenty of jeans that you love? Then focus on finding the right tops to dress them up or down. Are most of your clothes black or dark blue? Go for bold by adding bright or different colors to the mix. Want to make a statement? Look for unusual patterns or contrasts—maybe even a style you don't usually wear.

Thrifting has a lot to offer guys, too, from hats, jackets, and jeans to sporting goods and electronics.

Jewelry and Accessories

Shopping for jewelry, sunglasses, shoes, and handbags can be the ultimate thrifting adventure. Many of these items are one-size-fits-all. That means you don't have to hit the dressing rooms to try them on. Most thrift stores have plenty of mirrors scattered throughout the shop. Or bring some friends for feedback. Keep in mind that many accessories at thrift stores, especially at consignment shops, are either gently used or never worn at all. Many people overbuy and then sell off the pieces they don't want. It's not at all unusual to find a brand-new designer handbag at a more than reasonable price at your local consignment shop.

Accessorizing at thrift stores is a great way to unleash your inner fashionista without breaking the bank. Think about it: there's no need to stick with safe purchases at thrift stores because the prices are generally at least 20 percent less than what the new item would cost full price. Not sure you want to wear that flamboyant hat? No worries. Buy the crazy one for fun, and wear the safer one on those days when you're in a quieter mood. Wondering if you can really pull off those movie-star shades? Drop a few bucks, take them home, and test-drive them on your friends and family. You may be a hit!

Here are a few of the best accessories to look for at thrift shops:

- **Sunglasses.** Check the lenses for scratches, and make sure the sunglasses sit evenly on your face. Double-check that the lenses aren't prescription, and you're good to go.

- **Scarves.** Winter, spring, and fall—there's no reason not to change up a scarf collection each season when the price tag is only a few dollars per scarf. Small rips or stains can be easily hidden through clever knotting or folding styles.

Bags. From glamorous evening bags to camping backpacks, thrift-shop bags can help you get and stay organized. Make sure zippers and other closures work, check for holes in inner pockets, and look to see that straps or decorative items aren't missing or worn out.

Shoes. Thrift shopping for fancy prom shoes or other special-occasion footwear makes a lot of sense. So does thrifting for summer sandals and other shoes that aren't made to last. Look at the soles and heels of the footwear to see how worn they are. If the material is wearing thin, it may not be a smart purchase. If shoe straps are missing a buckle, you might want to think twice. But many shoes and boots come into the thrift store in great shape and can be a bargain.

Jewelry. Is there any better—or simpler—way to glam up your look? Thrift store jewelry selections are often more eclectic than you'd find at any full-price store. You might stumble across a truly vintage piece—or at least something outrageously huge, sparkly, or jangly. Go ahead and take a chance! Just be sure to inspect the piece carefully to make sure clips or other closures are in place and in working condition. Check that beads or other small pieces aren't missing and that any elastic that holds a piece together is still in good shape. And make sure the piece fits. Some bracelets can be super small, and not all earrings stay in place very well, especially if they are big.

Furniture and Home Goods

Thinking about redecorating your bedroom or your study? From lamps, picture frames, and wall hangings to beds, dressers, desks, bookcases, and bed linens, you can find everything you need at a thrift store.

Vintage or antique accessories, such as old phones and typewriters, record players and goofy toys, can be great accent pieces. Secondhand organizing supplies are also handy. Get sorted out with desk caddies, bins, trays, jewelry boxes, tool chests, or just about any other organizing container you could want.

Ask around to find local thrift shops that carry items for the home. You'll notice that many thrift and consignment stores only sell clothing. But at least one shop in your area probably has a small home goods section at the back of the store or in the basement. You'd be surprised by the bargains you can find there, because serious hunters don't always look at stores with small collections. But some thrift stores specialize in larger furniture items with a wide selection. Other places are crammed floor to ceiling with smaller gems such as lamps, vintage knickknacks, artwork, picture frames, tools, and other fun items.

So how do you judge the quality of home goods in a thrift shop? Start by thinking about the quality of the materials. The best items to thrift are made from durable materials such as metal, hard plastic, or solid wood. These materials make desk accessories, organizing items, lamps, picture frames, tools, and similar goods prime thrift fare. When looking at bed linens, keep an eye out for spots and tears. For fabric-covered items such as decorative pillows or comfy chairs, stick with fabrics made from natural fibers. The deeper or smoother the fabric, especially if it's made from polyester or another artificial fiber, the more likely it is to hold old spills and smells that are difficult, if not impossible, to remove. Stay away entirely from items such as fuzzy rugs or stuffed animals. They can hold dirt, odors, dust mites, and germs.

When you're judging furniture, kitchenware, tools, or artwork, look for labels or other signs of the company that manufactured the piece. Dishes and pottery, for example, are typically stamped on the back or bottom with the name of the manufacturer or the artist. Paintings and sketches are usually signed by the artist. High-quality furniture manufacturers generally mark their pieces with a label or a stamp of some kind. Look in drawers or underneath the piece to see if it has a label.

The age of furniture, decorative pieces, or tools has a huge impact on quality and how well they will stand up over time. The craftsmanship that went into the manufacture of older furniture items was of a higher quality than in more recent years. So were the materials. For instance, a desk or a chair that was made before the 1970s is almost always going to last decades longer than a similar piece of newer furniture. And boxed or ready-to-assemble furniture is much less likely to hold up over time. So before purchasing a larger item, take the time to give it a test-drive. Sit on a chair or couch, open all the drawers in a desk, and check to make sure table legs are steady. Remember that wood can stand up to many dents and scratches—but if you see cracks or warping, take a pass.

Sports and Recreational Equipment

From football and fishing to skiing and scuba diving, sports can go hand in hand with thrifting. Many types of gear—think baseball bats, skis, and hunting stools—are extremely durable and long-lasting, which makes them

Thrifters can find great deals on sporting equipment. But before purchasing, be sure to inspect gear, take the bike or other vehicle for a spin, and ask the seller about any imperfections to make sure you know what you're getting.

great secondhand purchases. Always take the time to inspect equipment carefully. Try on any clothing or footwear such as ice skates, ball gloves, or jerseys. Some stores will even let you try out some larger purchases to make sure they work for you.

Other sporting goods can be surprisingly fragile. Bicycles are a good example. You can easily find a bike for a bargain price, but it'll require a little effort to make sure you're getting a good deal. A top-of-the-line set of wheels that's only a couple of years old can cost less than half the price of a new bike. If you're looking for a simple beater bike to help you get around for a few weeks, you can sometimes find a bike at a thrift store

Throw a Party Using Thrift-Shop Finds

Do you have a special event coming up? Or are you looking for an excuse to invite your friends over? Throwing a party using thrift-shop finds can be fun—and surprisingly cheap. Just a few decorating and serving items can become centerpieces for any gathering. Try starting with a vintage theme such as 1950s Hollywood (think Marilyn Monroe) or 1970s disco. Here are a few ideas to get your party started:

- A random selection of plates and glasses is fun to mix and match. Or look for a matching set, which may cost less than the same number of paper plates and cups.

- Same goes for silverware and serving dishes. Mix and match—find a few great patterns or colors to use together.

- Serving dinner or snacks? Look for sheets or curtains in cool patterns to use as a tablecloth. Thrifts also carry vintage cloth napkins, which add character.

- For extra flair, see if you can score a vintage record player and vinyl records.

- Liven up the party scene with funky vases, candleholders, lamp shades, and other decorative theme-based trinkets from the thrift store.

for $25 or less. A reputable seller can help out either way. A good used-bike dealer will tell you about the bike's condition, describe any recent or still-needed repairs, and let you take a test-drive.

Thrifty Gifts

Looking for a birthday present for your oldest and best friend? Maybe you wish you had some serious cash to drop on something that would knock your friend's socks off. But even if you don't have much in the bank, you can shop for some pretty spectacular gifts at thrift shops.

Start by thinking about the person you're shopping for. What's unique about that person? What's this person's absolute to-die-for passion? Is it music, fashion, basketball, or maybe dogs, traveling, or skateboards? It probably won't take too long to come up with a gift theme.

Once you have a specific idea, scour the aisles until you find it. For example, do you have a friend with a thing for funny shoes or crazy mugs? Hit the thrift and consignment shops. Do you have a friend who's into vinyl records? They are making a comeback, and thrifting can be the way to contribute a record to the friend's collection. When buying vinyl, watch for scratches, breaks, and water damage. Or maybe your brother is bonkers for baseball. Look for some cool old team pennants for his wall. Or find some vintage baseball cards and a cool display frame. Better yet, get a photo of him—or his idol—playing his favorite position. Then go thrifting for the perfect picture frame and, voilà—a hall-of-fame gift.

As part of thrift shopping, go online to find out which stores are most likely to have what you're looking for. Many thrifting sites have a social-networking component too. Join the conversation to learn more.

CHAPTER 4
Tips for Better Thrifting

You don't have to be an über-shopper to land some great thrift-store finds. Following a few simple tips can make thrifting excursions super successful. And after hitting a few thrift shops, you'll probably be able to add to this list.

Do a Little Research

For first-time thrifters, make sure the stores you plan to visit carry the items you're looking for and are in your price range. If you know people who thrift, ask about their favorite spots as well as any tips they have. It's also easy to dig up info on the Internet. Many thrift stores, even smaller ones, have their own websites, where you can preview their collections, find out about the store's hours, sign up for a newsletter, or get linked to their Facebook page or Twitter feed. You can also visit review websites such as yelp.com or tripadvisor.com to see what other thrifters have to say about the stores on your list. And if you and your family are going on vacation, use the Web to learn about thrifting opportunities in your destination.

Plan a Thrifting Day

Looking for a fun way to get together with friends—and make some great thrift discoveries? A thrifting day might be just what you need! Here are some simple steps to help you build a thrift day to remember:

A few days ahead of time. Decide how many people your thrifting party will include and who you want to invite. Find a time when everyone's available. Decide together how many stores to hit, whether the thrifting expedition will have a certain theme or focus, and exactly how long to keep at it. Taking the bus or subway? Riding your bike? Make a plan for getting there. And know your shopping budget. Decide how much cash to take, or touch base with an adult about credit card use.

The night before. Check in with your thrifting companions to confirm plans. Make sure you all know where and when to meet.

That morning. Eat a good breakfast and collect whatever you'll need for your thrifting trip. Take along some reusable shopping bags to hold purchases. Also, leave the high heels and fancy outfits at home. When you're planning to try on clothes at a thrift store—which may or may not have a comfy changing room— you want to be able to take clothes off and put them back on quickly, without the hassle of too many buttons or zippers or multiple layers. Keep it simple!

If you set goals for thrift shopping, you'll be more likely to make good choices. But stay on the lookout for surprise finds. Some gems are lying around where you least expect them!

If you're looking for particular items, you can find a wealth of specific information online. For sporting gear, furniture, and many other items, you can research the best-quality brands and read user reviews to help narrow your search—and boost your odds of finding bargains. Look for specific tips about judging the quality and condition of items. Hunting for vintage fashion? Research trends from various decades and how people pulled their looks together before you hit the shops. You can also find out which brands were popular and which have stood the test of time.

Have a Game Plan

It's always a good idea to have a plan before thrifting. Your game plan might be as specific as "I need to find a belt for my new jeans." If you don't have anything definite in mind, your plan might still have broad guidelines: "I'm only looking at stuff for decorating my room" or "I am NOT buying another pair of black pants today!" Whatever the plan, leave room for a little adventure. Spot a pair of fab earrings or a cool baseball cap for only $3? Grab them while you can. Treasures don't stay on the floor long—they most likely won't be available on your next trip.

Let the Creative Thoughts Flow

Mentally prepare with images of the styles and items you're looking for. If you're shopping for clothes, take a quick browse at Pinterest boards or online style blogs. Flip through fashion magazines or visit your favorite overpriced store for great ideas to work toward as you thrift. Thinking about hitting the vintage shops? Watch a few classic movies or TV shows or look at online photos of style icons from earlier decades. Looking for furniture or home items? Blogs, magazines, and TV shows can be inspirations for interior design. Need sports equipment? A quick Web search can help you learn which brands your idols favored—and which ones to avoid!

Shopping Personality

What is your shopping personality? Some shoppers love to go as a big group—the more people, the more fun. For these shoppers, it's sometimes more about the hangout time than the purchases. Others like to go with one or two trusted confidants. You know who they are—friends who will tell the truth when you ask "How do I look?" Other shoppers like to go solo and get lost in their own, private shopping world. They don't want the distraction of friends or family when they're engaged in the serious business of shopping. If you're not sure about your style, schedule a few different thrifting trips to see which suits you best.

Take Your Time

Thrift shopping can be time consuming. Shops may not have what you're looking for, so you may need to hit more than one store. The outlet may be huge, crammed with shoppers (and not enough dressing rooms!) and with lots of racks and bins to go through. Feeling stressed out about time has been the downfall of more than one thrifter. Avoid this pitfall by selecting a day of the week and a time when you have at least a couple of hours—or more, if you really want to go full out. You might not need it, but you'll be glad to have it just in case.

Fuel Up

Shopping requires energy. And a tired shopper is not a successful shopper. Nor is a thirsty, hungry, or stressed-out shopper. Make sure you're prepared by freeing up enough time, getting enough sleep, and eating some protein before you head out. Planning to hit more than one store? Throw a small snack or a bottle of water in your bag so you don't end up spending your shopping money on body fuel.

Chat with Salespeople

This isn't always possible when stores are super busy, but if you get the chance, you can learn a lot from the people who work there. Ask them if they've seen any unique items come into the store recently. They may be able to keep an eye out for a particular piece you've been looking for. Ask them what their favorite stuff is or what the store specialty is. Some stores feature "Staff Picks" or "Staff Style Displays." Salespeople also know which days of the week the store receives shipments or donations and where they come from. (You can also check the website for this information.) And staff members know who shops at the store, which is another way to learn more about a shop's personality and style. Be sure to check about store specials too. Most thrift shops have sales, whether monthly, biannually, or on different days of the week. Some even have student days when all students get an extra discount.

Look for sales at secondhand stores. Many have seasonal discounts or pricing structures that reduce prices after a certain period of time.

Thrifting Limits

The thrifting experience comes in many shapes and sizes, and not every single one works for every single shopper. For example, Goodwill Outlets dump leftover donations from other Goodwill stores into a giant bin, leaving it up to shoppers to pick through items. To some hard-core bargain hunters, this is the ultimate in fun ways to find a treasure. To other shoppers, digging through bargain bins is slow torture. If you fall into this category, best to stick to well-organized shops with theme-based displays. Or for an even easier approach, go with online thrifting. Targeted keyword searches will narrow down your options fast.

Protect Your Health

Speaking of thrift-store outlets where everything is dumped into large bins, many secondhand stores are full of dust and other allergens. To some people, this is a mild annoyance. But for shoppers with allergies or asthma, dust can trigger some pretty serious attacks. Some people are allergic to certain types of fabric or detergents. Be aware of what your body can tolerate. If you tend to get sneezy around dust, take some allergy medicine before thrifting. And remember, no bargain is worth a trip to the hospital if dust triggers asthma for you. If so, a friend may be willing to shop for you.

Paying for It All

Make sure you have money for your purchases, even if you're not planning to spend a lot. And find out about a store or website's policies. Cash only? Credit cards only? Don't forget to ask about return policies too. Many places observe a no returns policy or have a very narrow set of guidelines for making returns.

Comparing Prices

Almost always, thrift stores offer good deals. But not all offer the same value. If you're looking for something very basic—jeans, picture frames, or a desk chair—check out the selection and prices at a few stores. Another way to make sure you're getting the best value possible is to start your hunt at the lowest-priced store in your community and work your way up to more selective consignment shops. Say you absolutely must have a black sweater for Friday night. Sure, you may be willing to pay twenty dollars or more for it, but what if you could get it for five or ten dollars? Hit a huge Goodwill or Salvation Army store first, and see if they have what you're looking for at the price you want. If not, try a smaller thrift store where you might pay a little more. If you're still striking out, it may be time to hit a more expensive consignment shop.

Take Advantage of the Season

The best deals on clothing items usually pop up in the season they're not meant for. For example, great deals on winter sweaters are not unusual in the summer. Looking for a new swimsuit? Try thrifting for it at the end of the swimming season. This makes sense when you think about it. At the beginning of summer, many people go through their winter wardrobes and donate items. Ditto for when it starts to get cold. So next time you're thrifting, look for outfits for the next season. What to do when you get home with a cute bikini or a snazzy pair of swim trunks in January? Up to you. Put it away for the summer—or throw a midwinter beach party!

Treat Yourself

Think you might never work up the nerve to wear that fuchsia-colored coat or those plaid vintage trousers? As long as it won't break the bank, go out on a fashion limb and buy them anyway. Who knows? Maybe that over-the-top item will become your fashion signature. If not, and you never wear the thing, donate it back.

Go Often!

Thrift-store merchandise turns over fast. No matter how many hours you've spent combing through the racks at your local store on any given day, you're practically guaranteed to see totally new items a week later. You can't always count on finding exactly what you're looking for on the day you're looking for it. But you can usually make a long-term goal work out if you're patient. A good way to make sure you get early dibs on new arrivals is to make a note of when stores put out their new merchandise. Get there when the store opens, even a little earlier if the store is super popular. Or ask a salesperson to give you a nudge when the item you're looking for comes in. Make a habit of regularly checking websites and social media to keep track of trends and new arrivals at your favorite shops and online sites.

CHAPTER 5
Upcycling Thrift-Shop Treasures

Ready to make the most of thrift-shop finds? Then it's time to upcycle. Upcycling is the art of making something new from something old. It's half-crafting and half-recycling, part-creative and part-green. Mostly, it's fun!

Get Creative

With upcycling you can be as creative as you want to be. Starting from scratch—from an actual pile of discarded junk—allows for dreaming, inventing, and building an entirely new or greatly improved product. Say you hit the thrift store and come home with what you thought was a to-die-for mint-green silk blouse. Then you notice it's actually kind of gross. How did you miss those stains on the collar? It's a little too tight. And mint green never was your best color. What were you thinking? But no worries. That blouse is ripe for upcycling. How about a summery scarf instead? Or a lightweight headband? Maybe even a belt? You can probably think of ten other ways to reuse that silk. Remember, too, that clothing isn't the only thing to upcycle. Some of the most imaginative upcycling projects involve small home decorations and gifts.

But what if you're not the naturally creative type? Upcycling is still a can-do project, with tons of helpful ideas and websites to inspire and to provide step-by-step how-to information. For beginners, it's smart to start with something that can be completed easily in a couple of hours or an afternoon. If you're already an expert, you can launch into a days-long or even weeks-long project. Some upcycling projects require skills and materials many people already have—think needle and thread, hot glue, or paints. Don't have many craft skills? No problem—you can learn as you upcycle, take classes, or invite a crafty friend to show you the ropes.

upcycling Thrift-Shop Gems

A quick search through Google, Pinterest, or YouTube will uncover hundreds of ideas for upcycling projects that start with a trip to the thrift store. Below are a few very basic ideas for items you can easily upcycle into something else. See how many more ideas you and your friends can come up with.

Vintage scarves. We're not talking vintage Hermes scarves from a designer consignment store. We're talking a bundle of old scarves from a Goodwill Outlets store or a church thrift shop that costs just a few dollars for the whole bunch. Cut them up, hem them, and use the fabric patches to decorate T-shirts, lightweight sweaters, or cloth handbags. Or sew all the scarves together to make a bedspread, curtains, or pillow covers for your room. Mix and match crazy patterns or stick with one color palette for some fun looks.

Picture frames. Frames are something that many thrift stores carry in bulk. Don't worry about the shape they're in because you're going to refinish them. Grab a few and be creative. With a can or two of spray paint from your local hardware store, paint several differently shaped frames the same color, or paint a few of the similar frames in different colors to group together. Try splash painting for a more random look. You can also glue-gun textured objects such as beads, shells, rocks, buttons, or assorted small stuff from the toolbox around the frame. Or use the glue to cover the frames with fabric (remember those scarves?) or with colorful strips of construction paper or from funky paper shopping bags. Frame favorite photos or artwork or baseball cards in the newly revitalized frames. They make great gifts for friends and family.

Silverware. Sure, vintage silverware is cool at a vintage theme party. But there's a lot more to make from old silverware. You can easily bend a spoon or a fork into a chunky bracelet, using a butane torch if necessary (with adult supervision, of course). Or get a little more adventurous by taking a few matching or mismatched pieces and bending them into hooks for coats or for your necklace collection. With a metal drill, screw the handles into a piece of wood to make a hook rack. An adult can help you mount the rack on a wall or a door.

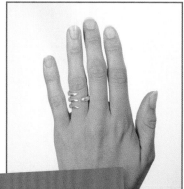

A tiny appetizer fork makes a funky ring.

Sweaters. Thrift-shop sweaters can offer the most awesome material for upcycling projects. Think pillows, doggie sweaters, fingerless gloves, or even a patchwork sweater quilt or lap blanket. Of course, you can always upcycle the sweater itself by adding patches, embroidery, buttons, or whatever strikes your style fancy to hide imperfections in the sweater.

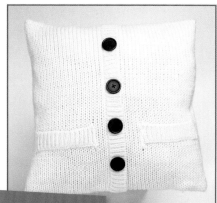

A sweater can be upcycled to make a decorative pillow.

Activity: One Sweater, Three Accessories

Here's a super-easy way to make three accessories out of one old sweater.

What you'll need:
- a pullover sweater with a pattern or a color you like, with some elasticity in it for making slightly stretchy accessories
- scissors
- a needle and thread
- decorations such as beads, fabric flowers, and colored thread

What you'll do:

1. On a work surface, lay your sweater out flat and cut off the arms, following the seams that connect the sleeve to the body of the sweater. Hem the seam where you cut, and you have leg warmers. Keep the smaller end, which was once near the wrist, at your ankles and pull up from there.

2. With your sweater still lying flat, cut a 2- to 4-inch (5- to 12-centimeter) band from around the neckline. Hem on all sides, stitch the ends together, and you've just made a headband. Sew on beads or other small baubles to decorate.

3. Cut off the bottom half of the sweater, starting just below the armholes. Hem the seam you've just cut and you've got a circle scarf!

Activity: Recycled-Book Tablet Cover

This fun tablet cover adds personality to your device and disguises what it is to foil would-be thieves.

What you'll need:
- a hardcover book that is about 1 inch (2.5 cm) larger than your tablet on all four sides. When closed, the book should be about the same thickness (or slightly thicker) than your device.
- a pencil or a marker for tracing
- a utility knife for cutting neatly and precisely
- 2 to 3 colorful rubber bands that are large enough to wrap around your book, top to bottom
- a stapler

What you'll do:

1. Set the tablet face down in the middle of the first page of the book and trace around it. Then use the knife to carefully cut out the shape of the device, following the line you traced. Repeat on each page or for a small group of pages that's easy to cut. As you cut more pages, the book pages tend to open and the spine flattens. When you are cutting, make sure the spine is as straight as you can make it, so that it is positioned as it will be when the book is closed. Keep cutting out pages. You've cut the hole deep enough when you can fit your tablet neatly inside and it is flush with the first page.

2. Choose two or three colorful rubber bands that fit over your book from top to bottom. Staple them to the back of the book in two or three places to secure them. Then slip the bands over the front of the book to close the case. When you open the case, just slip the bands over the inside cover of the back of the book.

Activity: No-Sew T-shirt Bag

What you'll need:

- an old T-shirt. Use a child-size shirt for a small bag. Use a large adult T-shirt for a big tote bag. The shirt can have long or short sleeves. You're going to cut them off anyway.

- scissors

- a large bowl (optional), approximately 7 to 9 inches (18 to 23 cm)

- a piece of white chalk

- decorative items such as beads, buttons, glue-on jewelry, or iron-on transfers

- a needle and thread

What you'll do:

1. On a work surface, lay your T-shirt flat.

2. Cut off the arms, leaving the seam attached to the body.

3. Cut out the neck in a rounded, scoop shape about 2 to 5 inches (5 to 12 cm) lower than the actual neck. To get a nicely even shape, place the bowl upside down on the fabric and trace the outside edge of the bowl onto the T-shirt with a piece of white chalk. Or you can just eyeball it and cut the scoop freestyle.

4. To make the fringed bottom seam, cut 1-inch-wide (2.5 cm) strips, starting from the bottom of the shirt and cutting upward about 4 inches (10 cm) into the shirt and through both sides of the shirt. Continue all along the bottom of the shirt.

5. For decorative flair, make double knots at the bottom of each strip. If you want a regular finish along the bottom of the bag, turn your shirt inside out before you tie. When you turn it right side out later, it will have a smooth bottom. If you want to have a fringe along the bottom of your bag, tie the strips together without turning the shirt inside out. You can also adjust the length of the strips for a longer or shorter fringe.

6. Time to decorate! Sew on beads or buttons. Apply glue-on bling or iron-on transfers. Or use a needle and thread for a little embroidery flourish. The sky's the limit!

If you have an entrepreneurial streak, you may want to resell upcycled and thrift-shop items. Research, preparation, knowing the rules, and patience are the keys to success.

CHAPTER 6
Selling Your Thrift-Shop and Upcycled Goods

Thrift shopping and upcycling have their own rewards: the thrill of the hunt, the fun of being creative, and a bunch of new stuff for not too much money. Remember that it's also possible to earn money from thrift-shop purchases and upcycled creations. Selling can be more time consuming than the original shopping and creative process, however. It also requires prep work, organizational skills, patience, background research, and people skills. If you love this kind of project, selling can be fun—and rewarding to your wallet.

To gauge whether upcycling will work as a small business, make one or two test items. See how much time, effort, and money you expend and if you can actually sell the items at an acceptable profit. If the answer is yes, then it's time to make more!

What to Sell?

Here are items that can often be found cheaply at thrift stores and resold for a good price without doing any upcycling at all:

- Brand-name clothing in good condition, especially women's or children's items

- Designer-label shoes, handbags, or wallets

- Books in good condition, especially kids' books, young adult or adult fiction, comic books, and graphic novels

- Vinyl record albums

- New, in-the-box toys

- New or nearly new electronics such as coffeemakers, clocks, speakers, or phone accessories

- Sports equipment in good condition

- Sports memorabilia such as cards, jerseys, and bobbleheads or other game-day giveaways

Buyers are also looking for upcycled creations such as these:

- Repainted furniture

- Repurposed or newly made jewelry

- Refinished picture frames

- Handmade dolls

- Decorative vases and other knickknacks

- Reimagined clothing and accessories

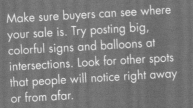

Make sure buyers can see where your sale is. Try posting big, colorful signs and balloons at intersections. Look for other spots that people will notice right away or from afar.

GARAGE SALE

What Can You Sell?

Just about anything is fair game for your resale business. Of course, not too many people want to buy just any old pile of junk you hauled home from a thrift store. But if you spend a little time selecting quality items, you can usually resell them for a profit. Buyers are sometimes looking for others to do the work of combing through thrift-shop aisles to find the fun deals, and they're willing to pay a little bit more for your time. Keep in mind, though, that you can get lost in the weeds by spending too much time, effort, and money for upcycling supplies—to the point where you can't really make a profit.

How to Hold a Sale

Holding a garage or yard sale is an ideal way to sell many things at once, as long as you're willing to do the work. You can sell thrift-store finds as well as secondhand items of your own that you're ready to let go of. If you have only a few items, see if friends or neighbors have enough to host a sale with you. Get started by following these steps:

1. Get permission from a parent or guardian. It goes without saying that this is the most important step. In advance, ask an adult at the home that's hosting the sale if they're okay with the plan. Some towns and cities also require a permit to hold a sale. Look online or ask an adult to check on this if you can't find the information yourself.

2. Pick a location. Choose a home or site that gets a lot of people traffic. A super-quiet neighborhood or a nook where no one goes is not going to lead to great sales. Involve the hosting adult in this decision. A driveway can be an easy spot to set up tables or other surfaces to display goods. If the adult isn't worried about harming grass, a lawn can be a good site too. Or if adults are willing to move cars and other big items, a garage is perfect especially if it rains. Live in an apartment building? Ask if the sidewalk is an option. If not, a local community center may have ideas for a nearby site that could work.

3. Pick a date and a time. Weekends are usually best for neighborhood sales. A common time frame is from about 7:30 or 8:00 a.m. to noon or 1 p.m. Pick spring or summer. No one likes a garage sale when it's freezing outside.

4. Enlist helpers. Ask friends or family members if they can help out by setting up, collecting money at the sale, keeping an eye on items, and clearing up after the sale is over. While you're at it, ask if they want to sell some items too. Generally, bigger sales attract more customers.

5. **Do some research about pricing.** Visit other garage sales ahead of time, or look up pricing for secondhand goods online. Websites such as eBay and Craigslist are good places to start. Think about volume discount pricing—that is, offering several similar items for the price of one. You can often end up selling items that might not have moved at all when you offer a volume discount. Two-for-one pricing is another strategy that can help sell items.

6. **Advertise.** Make about ten posters to hang in your neighborhood. Telephone poles at busy intersections are a good place to tack up or tape your signs. So are bulletin boards in neighborhood food stores, coffee shops, or hardware stores. (Don't forget to take down the signs when the sale is over.) Tell your family, friends, neighbors, and coworkers about the sale. Check the websites of neighborhood newspapers to see about placing an ad.

7. **Get change and make a plan for storing cash.** Since pricing at garage sales is usually pretty low, be prepared to make change. Have coins as well as plenty of $1 and $5 bills. Use a small box or money belt to store money during the sale.

8. **Select items to sell.** Choose things that are likely to sell. Make sure they are clean and in good shape. Few people want to buy a chair with no legs or a doll without a head.

9. **Mark prices on all items.** Use masking tape or stickers and a marking pen to indicate the price of each item. If you have items from different sellers, mark down sellers' initials on the masking tape. This makes it much easier to sort out profits at the checkout table. Be sure someone is available to keep track of sales at the event too. And if many of the things for sale are going to be the same price, make a simple sign to place next to items that all have the same asking price. Be realistic and base your price on the research you've done—not on how much money you dream of making.

10. **Set up your sale area and sort items.** Plan to do this the night before the sale if you're setting up in a garage. If the sale is outside, set up early in the morning, well before the sale starts. You'll want to set up tables or shelves for your items, have trash cans available, and have a supply of small bags if you're selling small items. Many shoppers arrive before a sale even starts, hoping to get dibs on the best things for sale. There's nothing worse than not being ready when they arrive.

11. **Be friendly, polite, and responsible.** Give customers your full attention if they have questions. Shoppers will sometimes choose not to buy something if they can't get the information they need. Have a plan for adult help if a customer is rude or upset.

12. **At the end of the sale, clean up everything.** This is part of being responsible. If you do a great job cleaning up, adults won't hesitate to give you permission the next time you want to have a sale.

13. **Count your money!** Count the money from the sale and figure out how much each seller has earned. Make sure to give each seller his or her earnings in a timely way.

How to Sell Online

Selling online is another way to turn a profit. But online selling is not for everyone. First, it requires a parent or guardian's permission—and help. Also, as with yard sales, it often takes a lot of prep work, attention to detail, and patience. Still, once you get the hang of it, it can turn into an efficient profit-making venture. With an adult partner, you can sell on large sites such as eBay or Etsy. Or you can place your own classified ads on sites such as Craigslist.

eBay

The world's largest marketplace of used goods is eBay.com. It's often the first place people think to check when they want to buy something. But competition is the name of the game here. Lots of people are selling the same items. The key is to sell a product that people want and at an attractive price that still offers you a profit. Do a little eBay research ahead of time to see what's for sale and at what prices. Enlist an adult to help. You must be eighteen or older to sell on eBay.

Keep in mind that eBay is huge. To quickly find what they want, many buyers search the site by brand names, so this can be the easiest way to sell your items. Remember, too, that eBay is a worldwide operation, and you'll have to ship almost all of your sales to your customers. That means you'll have to research the price of shipping to various parts of the world. You can either add that into your base price or charge a shipping fee to cover the costs. An adult can help you figure out the best way to factor in shipping costs.

If you become a dedicated eBay seller, you might have to factor taxes into your business plan. Have your adult partner help you check the Internal Revenue Service (IRS) website to find out if you need to file a tax return for your online income.

Etsy

Do you have upcycled goods or crafts you want to sell? Etsy.com is the go-to online marketplace for handmade crafts of any kind. Etsy is also a global site, connecting more than 70 million sellers and buyers. It started out as a marketplace for handmade crafts and has expanded to offer vintage clothes, decorations and crafting supplies, jewelry, handmade toys and knickknacks, and hand-sewn or -knitted clothes and blankets.

You don't have to pay to become an Etsy member—but you do have to be eighteen to sell on the site. That means enlisting a parent or guardian to help you sell here. When you register on Etsy, you'll be asked to come up with a unique username. You'll need a valid credit card from your adult partner to set up as an Etsy seller. Once you're set up, you're ready to take photos of your products, price them, and launch your sale. Sellers pay twenty cents to list each item for four months. When you sell an item, you pay 3.5 percent of your sale price to Etsy.

Craigslist

Craigslist.com is another huge online marketplace that can be seasy to use. However, just like eBay, Craigslist requires sellers to be eighteen or older, so you'll need an adult partner. Craigslist is divided into regional shopping sites, with more than seven hundred local Craigslist sites in seventy countries around the world. When selling through a local Craigslist site, buyers are usually responsible for picking up what they've bought, so shipping costs don't come into play.

Craigslist makes it easy to sell items on the website. Get started by clicking "post to classifieds" on the home page of your local Craigslist website. From there, follow the simple steps to post your ad. For personal safety, never meet customers at your home. Always arrange to meet them with your adult partner in a safe public space during the day.

The Recycle Circle

Thrifting is part of a larger recycling circle. Some items get bought, used, donated, and resold. Resold goods may in turn be bought, upcycled, sold, used, recycled, and sold again. Some people enjoy thrifting—scouring resale shops and websites for the perfect find. Others enjoy the creative act of upcycling. And others get the most satisfaction out of reselling their thrift or upcycled products. Whatever your personality, there's a part of the recycling circle that fits you best. Have fun!

Bibliography

Butterfield, Michelle. "26 Thrift Store Shopping Tips to Help You Score Awesome Stuff." *HuffingtonPost.ca*. October 16, 2013. http://www.huffingtonpost.ca/2013/10/16/thrift-store-shopping-tips_n_4108664.html.

French, Christina. *The Sweater Chop Shop: Sewing One-of-a-Kind Creations from Recycled Sweaters*. North Adams, MA: Storey, 2009.

Michael, Eric. *Fast Cash: Flipping Used Items: How to Make a Great Second Income by Selling Used Items from Garage Sales, Yard Sales, Thrift Shops, and Flea Markets*. CreateSpace Independent Publishing Platform, 2013.

Noel, Sara. "How to Shop Effectively at Secondhand Stores." *Sideroad.com*. Accessed July 1, 2014. http://www.sideroad.com/Budgeting/shop-secondhand-stores.html.

Willard, Joe. *Picker's Bible (How to Pick Antiques Like a Pro)*. Iola, WI: Krause, 2011.

For Further Information

The Art of Manliness: *"Thrifting: 5 Tips for Getting Top-Quality Products at Rock-Bottom Prices"*
http://www.artofmanliness.com/2011/01/14/thrifting-5-tips-for-getting-top-quality
-products-at-rock-bottom-prices/
Just for guys, this article offers tips and tricks to help male shoppers thrive at thrift shopping.

Blair, Barbara. *Furniture Makeovers: Simple Techniques for Transforming Furniture with Paint, Stains, Paper, Stencils, and More.* San Francisco: Chronicle Books, 2013. Want to learn how to dress up a thrift-store furniture find? Check out tons of cool projects in this book by upcycler extraordinaire Barbara Blair.

Cardon, Jenny Wilding. *ReSew: Turn Thrift-Store Finds into Fabulous Designs.* Bothelle, WA: Martingale, 2011.
Check out this fun guidebook for more than a dozen ideas for turning common thrift-store items into sassy, original finds.

Decades of American History series. Minneapolis: Twenty-First Century Books, 2010. Each book in this social history series for young adult readers includes a chapter devoted to the fashions of the decade. The series is a great starting point for thrifters who want to hone their awareness and knowledge of vintage styles.

DIY Network: *Upcycling*
http://www.diynetwork.com/upcycle-repurpose-refinish/package
Visit the DIY Network's website for great upcycling ideas. The site focuses on how to rejuvenate furniture, freshen vintage décor, and customize flea market finds.

Dodell-Feder, Jessica, and Karen Ziga. "How to Have a Money-Making Yard Sale." *This Old House* magazine online. http://www.thisoldhouse.com/toh/photos/0,,20516775,00.html
The online magazine companion to the popular public television show of the same name, *This Old House* offers twelve basic tips for creating a successful yard sale.

Federal Deposit Insurance Corporation: "Start Smart: Money Management for Teens" http://publications.usa.gov/USAPubs.php?PubID=5983
Buying and selling thrift-shop items is all about money management. Make sure you're being smart with your money by checking out the tips in this pamphlet for teens.

Junk Market Style
http://junkmarketstyle.com/
Ready to update your bedroom lamp shade—or remake your room entirely? Get hundreds of creative ideas for upcycling projects at this website, which collects ideas from users around the United States.

ModCloth
http://www.modcloth.com/
Searching for vintage or retro looks? ModCloth specializes in trendy retro looks for girls and women. It also offers lots of used goods, from vintage candleholders to 1950s eyewear.

Spencer, Lara. *I Brake for Yard Sales: and Flea Markets, Auctions, Thrift Stores, and the Occasional Dumpster.* New York: Stewart, Tabori, and Chang, 2011.
Learn the secrets of *Good Morning America* coanchor Lara Spencer, who has a passion for secondhand shopping.

Stocker, Blair. *Wise Craft: Turning Thrift Store Finds, Fabric Scraps, and Natural Objects Into Stuff You Love.* Philadelphia: Running Press, 2014.
Based on the popular blog of the same name, *Wise Craft* offers great upcycling ideas.

The Thrift Shopper
http://www.thethriftshopper.com/
Enter a zip code at this one-stop thrifting site to locate thrift, vintage, and consignment shops in your neighborhood. It also includes user reviews and discussion forums on thrifting issues.

Vazquez, Lilliana. *The Cheap Chica's Guide to Style: Secrets to Shopping Cheap and Looking Chic.* New York: Gotham, 2013.
Based on the CheapChicas.com site, this book offers great ideas for building a stylish wardrobe without breaking the bank.

Weber, Lauren. *In Cheap We Trust: The Story of a Misunderstood American Virtue.* New York: Little, Brown, 2009.
This entertaining and informative overview discusses American thriftiness, starting in prerevolutionary days and moving into the environmental concerns of the twenty-first century.

WGBH Educational Foundation: *Antiques Roadshow*
http://www.pbs.org/wgbh/roadshow/
Check out the website companion to the Emmy Award–winning television show that's devoted to finding and selling treasures of all kinds. The website has options to view episodes online, find Tips of the Trade, and peruse the Expert Library. It's a great site for learning more about how to assess the quality of a wide range of items.

Index

Photo Acknowledgments

The images in this book are used with the permission of: Backgrounds: © Mario7/Shutterstock.com (green floral pattern), (black floral pattern); © Mr Doomits/Shutterstock.com (plaid); © zroakez/Shutterstock.com (kanok pattern); © BrankaVV/Shutterstock.com (rug pattern); © 19srb81/Shutterstock.com (seamless plaid); © Volodymyr Burdiak/Shutterstock.com (colorful sweater pattern); © caimacanul/Shutterstock.com (large floral yellow); © Elif Eren/Shutterstock.com (red plaid background); © LanKS/Shutterstock.com (yellow fruit background); © Gyvafoto/Shutterstock.com, p. 2; © TerraceStudio/Shutterstock.com, p. 3; © gillmar/Shutterstock.com, p. 4; © Jack Hollingsworth/Stockbyte/Getty Images, p. 4 (inset); © gillmar/Shutterstock.com, p. 5; © Gyvafoto/Shutterstock.com, p. 5 (top); © Xetra/Fotolia.com, pp. 5 (bottom left), 63; © Russ Ensley/Dreamstime.com, p. 5 (inset); © Ryan McVay/Photodisc/Thinkstock, p. 6; © Bluehand/Dreamstime.com, p. 7 (top); © Liligraphie/Dreamstime.com, p. 7 (middle); © Coprid/Shutterstock.com, p. 7 (bottom); © Raphye Alexius/Image Source/Getty Images, p. 8; © gillmar/Shutterstock.com, p. 10 (top); © artjazz/Shutterstock.com, p. 10 (bottom); © Ragnarock/Shutterstock.com, p. 11 (top); © Alija/E+/Getty Images, p. 11 (bottom); © Tim Graham/Glow Images, p. 12; © Gloria P. Meyerle/Dreamstime.com, p. 15; © Image Source/Getty Images, p. 18; © Burke/Triolo Productions/The Image Bank/Getty Images, p. 20; © Richard Levine/Alamy, p. 21; © Anthony Hall/Dreamstime.com, p. 24; © Alina Cardiae Photography/Shutterstock.com (plaid pattern), p. 25; © Pawel Gaul/E+/Getty Images, p. 26; © Raphye Alexius/Image Source/Getty Images, p. 27; © Viktoria Gavrilina/Shutterstock.com, p. 28 (top); © Kaya/Shutterstock.com, p. 28 (bottom); © Ragnarock/Shutterstock.com, p. 29 (top); © iStockphoto.com/ewastudio, p. 29 (top middle); © Karkas/Bigstock.com, p. 29 (middle bottom); © Nuttakit Sukjaroensuk/Dreamstime.com, p. 29 (bottom); © Jacek Chabraszewski/Shutterstock.com, p. 31; © belchonock/iStock/Thinkstock, p. 32; © Hill Street Studios/Blend Images/Getty Images, p. 34; © iStockphoto.com/john shepherd, p. 35; © Andy Medina/E+/Getty Images, p. 38; © alenkasm/iStock/Collection/Thinkstock, p. 42; © Kaya/Shutterstock.com, p. 43 (top); © gillmar/Shutterstock.com, p. 43 (bottom); © Todd Strand/Independent Picture Service, pp. 44 (all), 45 (all), 47 (all), 48, 49; © Elena Kharichkina/Shutterstock.com, p. 46 (books); © Steve Ryan/Taxi/Getty Images, p. 50; © www.reinhartstudios.com/Moment/Getty Images, p. 52; © LanKS/Shutterstock.com, p. 58; © Alex Staroseltsev/Shutterstock.com, p. 59; © Giuseppe Porzani - Fotolia.com, p. 61; © nadi555/Shutterstock.com, p. 62; © artjazz/Shutterstock.com, p. 64.

Font Cover: © Alex Staroseltsev/Shutterstock.com (clock); © LanKS/Shutterstock.com (books); © Karkas/Shutterstock.com (necklaces); © nadi555/Shutterstock.com (brooches); © MichaelJayBerlin/Shutterstock.com (price tag); © artjazz/Shutterstock.com (lamp); © Gyvafoto/Shutterstock.com (frame); © TerraceStudio/Shutterstock.com (fedora hat); © elen_studio/Shutterstock.com (rings); © X-etra/Shutterstock.com (shoes); © Giuseppe Porzani/Fotolia.com (suitcase); © iStockphoto.com/ARSELA (dress); © iStockphoto.com/connect11 (purse); © iStockphoto.com/chengyuzheng (boots); © Gyvafoto/Shutterstock.com (records).

Back cover: © Nuttakit Sukjaroensuk/Dreamstime.com (vintage arm chair); © gillmar/Shutterstock.com (square gold frame). © Kues/Shutterstock.com (yellow floral).

About the Author

Sandy Donovan is a writer and thrift shopper who's written many books for teens on topics as varied as money and economics, history and politics, famous people, and famous events. She lives in Minneapolis, Minnesota, with three other writers: her husband and their two sons. She also lives with Carl the gecko, who is neither a writer nor a thrift shopper.